D1015718

THINKING
HISTORICALLY

THINKING
HISTORICALLY

Narrative, Imagination, and Understanding

Dennie Palmer Wolf, *Coordinating Editor*,

Robert Orrill, *Executive Editor*

Thomas C.
(Tom) Holt

College Entrance Examination Board, New York, 1995

Tom Holt is Professor of History, University of Chicago.

Dennie Palmer Wolf is Director, PACE (Performance Assessment Collaboratives for Education), Cambridge, Massachusetts.

Robert Orrill is Executive Director, Office of Academic Affairs, the College Board, New York.

The College Board is a national nonprofit association that champions educational excellence for all students through the ongoing collaboration of more than 2,900 member schools, colleges, universities, education systems, and associations. The Board promotes—by means of responsive forums, research, programs, and policy development—universal access to high standards of learning, equity of opportunity, and sufficient financial support so that every student is prepared for success in college and work.

Researchers are encouraged to express freely their professional judgment. Therefore, points of view or opinions stated in College Board books do not necessarily represent official College Board position or policy.

Single copies of Thinking Historically can be purchased for $12.00. Orders for five or more copies receive a 20 percent discount. Payment or purchase order should be addressed to: College Board Publications, Box 886, New York, New York 10101-0886.

Library of Congress Catalog Number: 89-082712

ISBN: 0-87447-537-6

Printed in the United States of America.

9 8 7 6 5 4 3 2

Contents

Foreword

*T*hinking Historically is one of a series of publications initiated by the College Board's Office of Academic Affairs. The books in this series address what many observers recognize as the central problem in significant educational change: the work of teaching all students, not a few, how to become competent thinkers (Resnick and Klopfer 1989). This work brings into existence a new conception of the place of thinking in the high school curriculum. Rather than being treated as a special, separate, and final skill, thinking will become the substance of the most basic classroom activities for all students in all subject areas. This series is designed to convey through discussion and example how many teachers are already making this concept a reality in their classrooms—how, that is, they make even ordinary moments occasions of thought for their students.

Thinking Historically focuses specifically on how one university teacher, Tom Holt of the University of Chicago, undertakes to work with students so that they actively question and imagine, not just memorize names and dates. Holt's narrative account of his work invites high school teachers to use his example to reconsider their own practices, most especially as it bears on the question of how the history classroom nurtures what has been called "a disposition to engage in thinking" (Resnick and Klopfer 1989). Other books in the series address thinking in mathematics, science, the arts, English and foreign language. Each explores how immersion in knowledge is required for thinking. All of the books, however, draw on both cognitive research and actual instances of classroom practice to convey how thinking should not be an activity that comes late in the curriculum after the acquisition of content, but rather is integral to successful learning in even the most commonplace and basic classroom situations. With deliberate purpose,

Thinking Historically and the other books in this series constitute a response to what Lauren Resnick has described as the urgent need "to take seriously the aspiration of making thinking . . . a regular part of a school program for all the population, even minorities, even non-English speakers, even the poor" (Resnick 1987).

ROBERT ORRILL

OFFICE OF ACADEMIC AFFAIRS

THE COLLEGE BOARD

Acknowledgments

B ob Orrill and Dennie Wolf suggested that I take on the assignment of preparing a short book on teaching higher order thinking skills to high school history students. I resisted the idea at first. Although, as a member of the College Board's History and Social Sciences Advisory Committee, I had supported the idea of such a series, I didn't think I was the one to do it, especially since I wasn't certain I knew just what "higher order thinking" was. (And I still don't like the term much.) Only after numerous conversations, especially with Dennie Wolf, did I begin to warm to the notion of writing a book based on my own teaching experience. With Dennie's promise that she would actively assist me through every stage of the planning and writing, I decided to take the plunge. She has kept her promise. She provided me with a fascinating set of transcripts from her interviews with high school students that, along with the materials and recollections from my own history class at Chicago, constitute the conceptual and textual core of this book. For those classroom materials I am indebted to Ira Berlin, Leslie Rowland, Joseph Reidy, and all the others who have worked on the Freedmen and Southern Society Project at the University of Maryland. Without these sources and Dennie Wolf's assistance, this book would have been a much thinner and poorer document.

My colleagues on the Social Science Advisory Committee— Carole A. Buchanan, Gregory Figgs, Michael Hartoonian, John R. Howe, and Hue-Tam Ho Tai—responded enthusiastically, creatively, and critically to an earlier outline, which fortified me for the task ahead. A special group of teachers, college and high school, read an early draft of the essay and then gathered to discuss it with me. Their positive responses and suggestions for improvements were much appreciated, although I could not incorporate all of them into the revised essay. I would also like to acknowledge students from Cambridge Rindge and Latin High School, Cambridge, Massachusetts; Concord Academy, Concord, Massachusetts; and South Vocational Technical High School, Pittsburgh, Pennsylvania. Thank you Dean C. Brink, chair, History Department of Seattle's Roosevelt High School; Gregory Figgs, social studies teacher at Lexington, Kentucky's Bryan Station High School; Kevin Jennings, history teacher, Concord Academy; Gale Justin, professor, City College of New York; Zachary Rubin, history teacher, Philadelphia Public Schools; and Beth Warren of Bolt, Beranek and Newman in Cambridge, Massachusetts. Professor Leora Auslander, my colleague in European history at the University of Chicago, took time to read the penultimate draft of the essay and reassured me that she "liked it," which I took as high praise from someone who has thought long and hard about the discipline of historical analysis and writing. Bob Orrill got me into this and continued to give me unstinting support even when I suspect he became skeptical of whether it would ever get done or whether he'd like it much when it was. As my "publisher" in this project, I couldn't ask for more. A great deal of whatever success this book enjoys must be credited to these colleagues; the failures are mine alone.

Finally, Dennie Wolf would like to add a special thanks to the Mellon Foundation for its support of the Literacies Institute that made possible the interviews with the history students.

TOM HOLT

Editors' Introduction

High school teachers could find this small book startling. It is written by Tom Holt, a professional historian, who teaches at a prestigious university. In it, Holt thinks aloud about an undergraduate course he taught in which he and the students considered a set of familiar and less-well-known historical documents, asking large and difficult questions, such as, "What counts as freedom?" At first glance, Holt's experience seems remote from that of his colleagues teaching in high school. He does not face classes of 30 students, a single textbook, or the demands of "coverage"—everyday considerations for almost every high school history teacher. And yet, Holt speaks to, and not at, high school teachers, urging that the essential questions about teaching history are the same at all levels.

How can this be? Holt makes his case, not through pronouncements, but by providing a personal narrative of how he thinks about teaching history. By opening his practice to view, he invites high school teachers to reflect on their own teaching. This is a bold step. Teachers often say that what happens after they "close the classroom door" is their own business. But Holt leaves the door of his classroom open, asking other teachers to examine their assumptions by making his own visible.

What are some of the assumptions that Holt invites teachers to examine?

■ *Student misconceptions must be explored, not ignored.* Just like high school students, most of Holt's students come to class believing that history is a matter of time lines and treaties, getting or missing the date of the battle. He sees that an essential part of teaching involves drawing out and actively contesting these deeply entrenched views. Misconceptions, after all, are still conceptions; the hold they have on a student's mind can severely constrain how and what they are able to think. Thus, Holt begins student learning with "unlearning." He teaches them that to do history is not to memorize, but to question and to imagine. It is to go beyond facts toward the making of a narrative, with all the selection, empathy, and risk of a point of view that this implies. Historical thinking, he says, requires curiosity and a search for the paths of access, not just "getting things by heart." Thus, while he insists his students read the Emancipation Proclamation closely, Holt also wants them to read between the lines and to remember that the document was created and shaped by human minds. Behind its phrases are doubts, fears, visions, and beliefs. Reading it historically also means imagining what was not said, why, and how it might have been otherwise.

■ *Teachers must be models of mindfulness.* Even the best textbooks show students only one result of doing history. They are products, not processes.This leaves teachers with a critical responsibility. Holt points out that it is the teacher's mindfulness — the questions he raises, the way he wrestles with an issue, his own ability to enter the lives of another time — that will teach students what doing history means. A teacher must put himself on the line, struggle with the same matters that he puts before students. Answers are not "in the book," but come from the environment of thought that a teacher creates. Thus, teachers must find ways to make their thinking public, visible, audible — without prescribing its course or conclusions.

■ *Strong teaching involves values and choices.* Holt's classes are themselves implicitly experiences in narrative, not chronicle (Bruner 1986). On any given day, he selects and leaves out documents, he chooses the order in which they are read, he opens discussions with specific questions. The class itself becomes something of an example of a historical narrative in the making. Wanting to offer his students a genuine apprenticeship in history, Holt exposes the "seams" of the work, showing the way values and choices enter into it. There is nothing pat about the outcome. Such things as points of view, beliefs, the incompleteness of history — difficult as these matters may be — come into his conversation with students and the kinds of tasks he asks them to undertake. He talks about history, not as a record, but as the play of competing narratives — even if some students shift in their seats, resist discussion, or demand a simple statement of "what happened."

■ *A "basic skills" approach postpones learning.* Like much recent research in cognitive science, Holt's personal account challenges the notion that there are basic skills that have to be acquired before students can move on to "higher order thinking skills." In his course, he refuses to lay out the time line for Reconstruction first and save questions about conflicting definitions of freedom for later. Rather, he begins by asking students for their definitions of freedom and only then moves to an exploration of how conditioned these ideas are by historical experience. He insists that students take on what Barzun calls "the whole tangled mess"—historical facts, documents, secondary sources, the problems of evidence and interpretation—from the outset. Thus, he refuses an approach to teaching history that confirms students' misconception of it as the memorization of "someone else's facts." Instead, he insists that the study of history be an experience in authentic problem solving.

Holt is not alone. In fields as different from history as mathematics and foreign language, researchers and teachers recognize the damage done when students learn a subject through simplified exercises and drills in isolated skills. These are more like an inoculation against thinking than a preparation for it. Instead, the challenge is to provide students with genuine opportunities to think even as they first start out (Hirsch 1989; Resnick 1987; Resnick and Klopfer 1989; Silver 1990). This leads to a kind of history teaching that diverges from much of current practice. The usual assumption is, "Teach them the basics: the time line, the names; and later, if they're bright, add in the big issues." However, we are learning that the "basics" are those skills that, ironically, we have heretofore reserved for the end and saved for the few.

■ *The meaning of "higher order skills" must be reexamined.* When Holt pauses to think aloud about what doing history involves most, he nominates "questioning" and "imagining." Until recently, the customary answer would have been "inquiry, analysis, and synthesis." Again, Holt is not alone in seeing that we need to think of learning differently. Much of cognitive research insists that thinking is fundamentally inventive, not merely synthetic (Keller 1983; Gruber 1981; Perkins 1983).

Facts are not "irrelevant"; but they are only "data." And while data feed and illustrate, they do not engender. Thought comes first in finding a problem worth solving or a question worth pursuing: Darwin had to think outside the frame of creationism before he could assemble his Galapagos observations into a powerful pattern. Lorraine Hansberry had to imagine a theater very different from familiar European dramas as she worked out the lines and images of "Les Blancs." Similarly, seeking a history of Reconstruction requires questioning the official record, seeking out voices that have not been previously heard, and following intuitions that new or different evidence may be found in unorthodox places (Foner 1988).

Thought demands going beyond the information given—in having the imagination to assemble data into a narrative, a model, or a theory—in having the agility to work around the gaps. In this light, history does not look like a matter of simple detective work. It is more like scientific theory building than we are accustomed to thinking (Crick 1988). Like literature, it is also about creating possible worlds with conviction (Woodward 1989). Moreover, if all this is the case, teaching has to change. We have to ask, for instance, how students will learn to raise good questions, especially if more than half of what we ask in class simply sends them back to locate a name, date, or definition in the text (Wolf 1987). We have to ask how they will learn the imaginative aspects of history, if the lectures they hear, the texts they read, and the tests they take only hug the data.

■ *Authentic materials prompt thinking.* Holt's students pore over letters and diary entries, not just famous public statements like the Emancipation Proclamation. He doesn't provide them with a single authoritative text. His students piece together history from many places, some of them quite ordinary. In changing the very nature of the "text" in his class, Holt is one of many historians who insist that the historical record has been too narrow, too simply political, and too exclusive. He is arguing for a much more heterogeneous history that includes the journal of a freedwoman, letters of dispossessed plantation owners, daguerrotypes, and marriage records. In this light, he is in the company of educators in other fields who are arguing that we cheat students when we offer them vocabulary-controlled stories, "cookbook" lab experiments that are really only exercises in verification, and math problems that lack the noise and challenge of genuine mathematical questions (Mestre and Lochead 1990; National Council of Teachers of Mathematics [NCTM] 1989; Silver 1990).

This can open up history teaching. Teachers can, if they will, find materials in newspapers, in historical societies, or in oral histories. By introducing it undigested and "live," they put into student hands, not some picked-clean, smoothed over, canonized history, but something much closer to the raw materials for historical thought. Students, like historians, profit from finding ways to make such materials speak.

■ *Students know more than we think.* At this moment, it is fashionable to tally up all that students do not know: when the Constitution was written, who Nathaniel Hawthorne was, the incident that set off World War I (Cheney 1987; Hirsch 1987; Ravitch 1987). But as Holt points out, it is mistaken and unhelpful to think of students as ignorant or empty. Drawing on direct experiences with his students and interviews with high school students, Holt shows us that students bring to class their theories of history and powerful mythologies about freedom, rights, and access. Their views may be personal, rather than academic, and they may be unexamined, but they are what a teacher has to work with—to draw on and to push against.

Moreover, through interviews with high school students, Holt shows us that they know what it is to narrate (Labov 1972; Polanyi 1982). Every day they select and shape language so as to convince a friend, get a hall pass, make themselves heroes in their anecdotes. Intuitively, they know what it is to achieve an effect through language. Here Holt is making points that cognitive scientists and educators working outside history are also trying to convey. Students are anything but blank slates. Studies of science classrooms tell us that students' naive theories shape what they learn and what they resist (Mestre and Lochhead 1990). Work in foreign language learning shows how profoundly a student's world knowledge and first language can guide the acquisition of a second language (Hirsch 1989; Krashen 1981; Molinsky and Bliss 1980). The point is at once simple and demanding. We have to inquire into students' minds and find out what they believe and how they think, if we are to address either their misconceptions or draw out what is relevant in their experience.

All this is a great deal, but there is more. What he has produced is, in the best sense, full of provocation. In challenging himself and others to do better, Holt insists that there should be fundamentally no difference between work at the college and high school levels. The history usually reserved for the few, he says, is the history that ought to belong to all.

DENNIE PALMER WOLF

ROBERT ORRILL

CHAPTER 1

School History

When I first took history, I did not like it. The preponderance of dates, multiple-choice tests, and one-dimensional explanations left me mentally unchallenged. But later on when I took history again, I became fascinated with the process of historical inquiry which was totally different from my earlier experience and realized that I wanted to be a history major. —Janet D.

J anet's lament is not uncommon. All too often—in high school and in college—we introduce students to history as "dates, multiple-choice tests, and one-dimensional explanations," saving for "later" the compelling work of actually *doing* history. This is likely to be true especially in survey courses, in which all teachers confront the same problems: the tyranny of coverage and the enormous pressure to convey a given set of basic "facts." Janet echoes much contemporary criticism about what's wrong with history teaching and evokes a sigh of recognition from any historians who have had the experience of explaining to a skeptical inquirer exactly what it is they do and why it matters.

The problem is that everyone already knows what history is. Like Janet, they have all had a survey course, sometime, somewhere; and to know it was to hate it. Almost invariably it wins hands down as "most boring." All those dates, all those facts to remember. "Which battle turned the tide of the Civil War?" "Which President said . . . ?" "Just one damn thing after another," a cheeky undergraduate once told me. At the beginning of each new term, I confront a class full of Janets. "Do we have to remember dates?" "Will the exam be multiple choice?" Before I can teach them history, they have to unlearn what they think history is.

What do high school students think history is? What follows are excerpts from interviews with two students, the kind I would like to get in my college history courses. What they say reveals a good deal about how they think history works. Plainly put, they conceive of history as the ordering of already known facts into agreed-upon chronologies. They think of history as sealed off both from the lives of ordinary people and from questions about how the particulars of everyday life become the generalizations of historical knowledge. For many students, only a fiction writer shapes and interprets—not a historian. And above all, they think they are the consumers, not the makers, of history. It is there: fixed, final, and waiting to be read.

"Someone Else's Facts" versus Imagining History

Debbie is a senior at a vocational high school. Many of her classes aim at the kind of basic education we customarily offer to students who, we imagine, will become mechanics or office managers. And many of her classmates only want what it takes to write business letters or fill out forms. But in her last two years, Debbie has started to write in more than a routine way— possibly because of an English teacher who has offered her more than exercises and book reports. As a result, Debbie struggles some when she has to write a term paper on a historical figure, complete with footnotes and bibliography. In this conversation, Debbie reflects on her paper on Karl Marx, comparing it to a personal essay she wrote about the events surrounding her sister's death.

> *Interviewer:* How did you go about doing the writing?
>
> *Debbie:* Well, we went through lots of steps. First we got a list of topics that we were supposed to do cards on. Like his early life, his adult years, his family, his career, and his contributions, and then our evaluations. There was a different colored kind of card for each. And you filled them up for each. I started with his early life, and I wrote the notes on that. And then I did it for his adult life and his contributions, like that. Then when I had all the cards, I put it all

together. I had to write several drafts; she gave us about two or three weeks for the whole thing.

Interviewer: What was different about writing history?

Debbie: Having all these facts out there floating. I did a lot of reading; we had to have three books that weren't encyclopedias, so it was hard work getting the facts in the right order. I'd think I had finished with his early life and then I would come across something else that went in there. Or there were things that were a part of all his life, like his interest in politics, and that was hard to put in any one place.

Interviewer: But what was different about writing history? Say, as compared to when you write about events from your own life? Or when you write about something you have read?

Debbie: I didn't really know who Marx was, so the whole thing is someone else's facts.

Interviewer: Was there a part of it that caught your attention, where you would have liked to put in more time?

Debbie: It was interesting to me that he became so famous. The first time I opened up one of the books, I remember thinking, "Oh, I don't want to read this," and then thinking, "This is interesting, the people back then, they loved him, they thought he was so amazing, even if his views were so different from what they were used to." I thought, it was amazing that he could become famous with just ideas; he must have been very, very smart.

Interviewer: Did you think about writing about that?

Debbie: Well, that's just what I thought. [But] we had our outline from the cards, you know, the introduction, the early life, his contributions, those parts.

What strikes one immediately about Debbie's notion of history is her implicit image of "facts." They appear as the foundlings of human experience "out there floating" around waiting to be taken up. Or they are hard nuggets of the real dug out of books, "someone else's facts." The process of collecting facts seems separable somehow from the process of thinking. "It's not from my mind," she says. Transparent and self-interpreting, facts are looked up and put on cards, not constructed.

From Debbie's point of view, what she thinks about Marx is not important. How does she know? Because in the assigned outline there is no place, or no place that she understands, for the unanticipated questions. She is convinced that the puzzles she encounters with life from another time and culture are marginal, not central, to the process of reconstructing the past. Thus her own curiosity at the reasons for Marx's fame is trivial; it is only what she thought. The act of writing history, then, is merely an ordering process, much like setting the table for dinner. The ordering is self-evident: It is chronological. The facts march off in unvarying lockstep to the tyrannous drumbeat of Time: Marx was born; he had an early life; he had an adult life, including a family and a career; he made contributions; he died.

As the interview continues, Debbie compares her history writing to office work: It is hard and requires close organization. It is utilitarian, dry, formulaic. At the same time, she argues that her Marx paper is exactly what is implied by the term "report"—it is no more a place for imagination or engagement than is a business letter:

> *Interviewer:* But what do you think you learned about reading and writing about things in history?
> *Debbie:* Well, that it's a lot of hard work. You write down the facts, and then organize them, which is another lot of work. I think it helps you develop for the kind of writing, say, that you have to do in a business. Like if you have to write a letter. You might have to do some research, collect the facts, and then put down something in the end.

When asked if she thinks about this writing as creative, she answers:

> *Debbie:* Well, I am selecting what is important. It's not creative, though; it's facts that other people have already written about. I am just organizing them in my way. It's not from my mind. It's just my selection of what really happened back then.

Debbie goes on to explain what she means by comparing it with the essay she has been writing—oddly enough—about her own family's history. She reflects about the process of writing about the years when her sister was dying of leukemia:

Debbie: With my sister, it is all pulled from my mind. I mean my feelings have a big place. The Marx paper is all from books. I guess I have to invent so it's not just copying, you know, put it in my own words. But there is nothing unique. I am using facts that other people found out and know already.

Interviewer: But aren't you making a story about Marx where there was just a collection of facts before you came along?

Debbie: No, just organizing it. I can't make up anything. I can't put in my feelings, so it is very, very different. I like the other [essay about her sister] better. There I am making it myself. No one else ever did it. I would rather start from scratch where no one else has ever been. In the essay about my sister it is more of a challenge because you have to find the facts. With the Marx paper, you have the facts; you just have to put them together. In my own writing, I am introducing what happened into the world; that's not the case here. Everyone knows about Marx.

History, or at least school history, is not the place for feeling. How could chronologies and achievements move you? Nor is school history an occasion for discovery, insight, or imagination; only for finding and arranging the facts. How could you introduce anything new about Marx? It has all been written, hasn't it? Consequently, for Debbie, as for many students, history is only a summation; it cannot be a point of departure.

As she talks about finishing the essay on her sister's death, Debbie says she would have "about 10 more drafts." When asked why so many, Debbie describes, unwittingly, how a historical narrative works:

Debbie: Well, I realize I have to put more of when she is well into the story. Because otherwise all you do is see her when she is sick and then you would say to yourself, "Why is it a terrible thing that she died?" You need the contrast of what came before to really appreciate it. And what comes after when I could write about how we all changed—I think me and my sister changed, and my mother and father changed—I would put in how she loved going out with her friends and what she did and what she used to say. And exact memories like what we used to do at Christmas, in the morning. And how our house was so different after she died. That's the only way the person could really see what I lost. You need the comparison.

Interviewer: Would you tell it just like that, in order: first she was well, then she got sick, she struggled and died, and then the family changed?

Debbie: All I know is that I could do it lots of different ways. Like start at the beginning. Or start in the middle of when she is sick and work backward to before and ahead to when she is really dying and couldn't go outside even anymore.

Interviewer: So you don't imagine sticking to what happened in the order it happened?

Debbie: No, I think the point is to see which way works. I mean I would have to choose the way that I could do it, and the way that made it clear what I was trying to say about her life.

Interviewer: Well, but since it really happened, isn't that the one way to tell it?

Debbie: Well, no, not really, it's up to me. I might like working back and forth to the memories. That might work better. I would really have to try it to see.

There was only one way to tell the story of Karl Marx; but her sister's story can be told "lots of different ways." The facts here are not self-evident; their resonance, acceptance, and comprehension depend on the author's creative manipulation and insight. Here she can see that it makes a difference if the reader knows what her sister was like before her illness ("You need the contrast"). Here she realizes that it will be different if told chronologically or as a memoir or as a movement back and forth in time. No, the facts do not speak for themselves. Order alters meaning. It conveys to the reader what's important and what is not. To make sense, the narrative must have a point. So the correct way to represent the facts of that narrative is not through some slavish fidelity to their chronological order. As Debbie recognizes, the correct way is the one that will make it clear "what I was trying to say about her life."

Capital "P" People versus Questioning History

If Debbie lays out for us how students think history works, J.J., a 15-year-old sophomore, teaches us how students view history as distant from and irrelevant to the "real" content of ordinary lives. J.J, like Debbie, draws a sharp line between story and history.

> *J.J.:* History is just so general . . . and being general makes it really distant . . . and being distant can make it boring. And story, that is writing about characters . . . people.

> *Interviewer:* And history is not about people?

> *J.J.:* Not really . . . it is more about the general people; it's about the world. Capital "P" people. It's about The People, and other things are about characters or a person. And I want to write about a person, not people . . . and I don't want to write just a biography of a person; I want to be in their head and talk about what they do and how they think. [But] history is written from the outside.

> *Interviewer:* But some people who actually do history would say that that is exactly what it ought to be about . . . they might say that history can be about just what you have in your story here: 1962, Kirkwood, Missouri, and what the life of people was.

> *J.J.:* But you can't . . . that's not true . . . if we were writing a history paper about 1962, the teacher would want all these facts about specific events that happened. [She holds up stories.] These are unimportant events, not battles and V-days.

Interviewer: Wait, let's go back to this imagining . . . imagine you just decided to write a history paper about life in the early sixties in the Midwest. How would that paper be different from a story about Kirkwood?

J.J.: I would have to make it all general.

Interviewer: So give me a couple of sentences from it.

J.J.: [Reads paragraph of her story about a young girl slamming out of the front door of her house, translating it into what she thinks of as the language of history.] "Because of the situation and the way that . . . ninth-grade girls often felt during this period of time, they would probably slam the door out of pure frustration when angry with their mothers. This was because their mothers thought thus and so . . . as related to the way that they were brought up in this period of time. The daughters, having a conflict with that . . . " You know, it would be on the outside, general, boring, not a place to invent.

Like Debbie, J.J. has been drilled in the notion that classroom history is "about facts." Moreover, these are general facts in a way that is troubling to J.J. with her interest in the particular. In contrast with her stories, history texts are not about real people, and writing them involves no investment of self, no imagination or creativity or originality, no opportunity to get one's "two cents in." And although J.J. may be naive about the ultimate objectives of the historian's project—that it is to arrive at the generalizations about human experience based on the particulars of individual lives—intuitively, she raises insightful questions about that project nonetheless. She knows human life is detailed, events are ragged, and there are "many sides to a story." She knows that it makes a difference just who decides what's important in the story of the American people, or just who gets included in "the American people," or what "winning" the West meant. Who puts the story together? How is it done? And why? In essence, she wants to question and reflect on the "doing" of history.

J.J.: My teacher . . . he is always saying, "History is true," and I say, "You don't know that. How do you know? How do you know that some monk didn't come along and just change a few words because he liked it better?" Then he says, "But for history there is proof." "No, there isn't." And so the whole class always gets on my case, and they always get really mad when I say that . . . but . . . I don't think that history. . . I don't always believe it . . . because it can be so easily changed. What if there is one document saying, "Thus and so happened"? Maybe someone wanted it to happen and wrote it up that way; maybe it didn't really happen. And if a hundred people saw it, it could be that a hundred people wanted to see it. Maybe the hundred people saw it and all wrote it down according to how they really saw it happen, or they embellished it a little bit. So that can all change everything.

Interviewer: But what does your history teacher say when you ask those questions?

J.J.: He says, "But . . . " And then the other people in the class join in and say, "How could there be five different people in five different places in the world who all said the same thing?" And I say, "So?" Five people are five people; they are just people, and it's okay that it is a lie, and it is okay that there is a book called *The History of the World,* and it is okay that there are all these stories, but why are they more than stories? I don't get that. Just because they are *told* from an impersonal point of view, that doesn't make them true. Especially if the people telling the history are always the winners. I mean the people who died in the battle aren't going to be telling about it, so how do you know what really happened?

History is "about something that everybody already knows about." Students are simply asked to redigest someone else's thoughts. History is about important events, important people, "capital 'P' people." It is told by the winners. No wonder it's boring.

Debbie and J.J. show us the inchoate beginnings of two essential processes in historical thinking: creation and analysis—narration and questioning. But these same students are also clear about what we actually teach them: how to arrange someone else's facts and how to take the perspective of the winners as "the" record. But we could decide to do otherwise. For instance, would students' notions of history be different if they were given a chance to be historians? What if they were allowed to examine the raw materials of historical research on their own and come up with their own compelling accounts of the "facts"? What if they were regularly asked to take the fragmentary and incomplete evidence of history and construct a narrative that pursued a question and made a point? What if each student historian were allowed to encounter competing narratives about that same event? In other words, what if we offered students like Debbie and J.J. an apprenticeship in history that carried them beyond their intuitive sense for plotting and questioning narratives?

Designing such apprenticeships is not easy. It requires reflection, a search for materials, and experimentation. Even to begin, we have to ask ourselves:

■ What does being a historian involve? How could historians make their *way of working* and not just the content of their work visible to students?

■ Can students grasp what is being made visible?

■ If so, how can we help students take on the work of history in ways that are at once imaginative and rigorous? ■

CHAPTER 2

Being a Historian

We are all historians. History, after all, is past human experience recollected. Thus our own everyday experience is the substance of history: our individual life cycles, our family's or community's stories, the succession of generations. To construct coherent stories about this collective experience—something we all do—is to create histories. In some premodern societies—African and Native American come readily to mind—this function was formal and explicit. Stories of the origin and development of the group were passed on orally from one generation to the next; they were crucial components of the education of the young. Through such histories young people learned who they were and, implicitly, who they could become. The division of labor characterizing modern societies leaves this task to the professional historian and to history teachers in schools, but the task is not fundamentally different.

As a historian, I do what Debbie does when she puzzles out a shape for her sister's life and what J.J. does when she questions the materials of history. For like them, the professional historian brings to this task the collective product of who he or she is. Moreover, in the process of doing history, one can be changed, transformed by what one learns. Stories have power. The power to change things. Thus history is not dead but alive, alive in the sense that our collective memory is what provides the starting points for understanding our contemporary world. Alive also in the sense that through these narratives we make accessible certain ideas about human possibilities and foreclose others. For example, our narratives of origin—whether national, racial, ethnic, or familial—have inscribed within them notions about destinations. Witness some history titles: *The*

Growth of American Democracy, From Slavery to Freedom, The Bonds of Womanhood. In short, who we understand ourselves to have been plays a powerful role in shaping our ideas of who we might yet become.

History is not just battle swords, treaties, and revolutions. It is all around us. It is the common staple of books, movies, advertisements, and everyday media. It is invoked by political leaders to argue the policies they want adopted; by political pundits to show where those leaders are going wrong. The alleged errors of history, Munich, Vietnam, or Prohibition, have shaped public discourse for decades at a time. What is involved here, however, is more than a matter of the use and misuse of history. It is that inevitably we think in historical terms, consciously or unconsciously. We create stories that guide and resonate with how we think about our present.

All of this suggests that when we introduce students to history as an academic subject, we might take advantage of this fact by reversing the usual process. Rather than teaching them to be consumers of stories, "someone else's facts," we might better develop their critical faculties by letting them create stories of their own. One way to do this is by letting students work with the raw materials of history, the actual documents, letters, voting statistics, etc., from which professional historians construct their narratives. In the process they can be introduced to the essential skills a historian must cultivate, which is really simply a set of questions one puts to the materials or document. Is it a primary or secondary source; that is, is it produced by an eyewitness or participant, or by a commentator after the fact? What is the point of view of this source? How and why was this document produced, and how does that affect its trustworthiness? What are the document's silences? What does it leave out? What does it assume?

But breaking down or analyzing the document is only part of the task. The ultimate task is to use the document or documents to synthesize a narrative about an event or development. Why do I say narrative? Because history is fundamentally and inescapably narrative in its basic structure, even when it is not reported in a narrative form. Time is one of the essential dimensions that distinguishes history from most other studies of human behavior. For historians, almost by definition, the time dimension is an essential part of the explanatory process. And as philosopher Paul Ricoeur (1984) has shown, time and narrative are each intimately implicated in the other.

History is narrative also in the sense that it has a plot; it imposes order on past experience. Like fiction writers, therefore, historians work with 'plots," in their heads if not on their pages. There is a beginning, a middle, and an end. In history something is always developing, breaking down, emerging, transforming, growing, or declining. Otherwise, it's sociology.

The historian selects, arranges, and subordinates the elements of historical experience in keeping with some temporal order that is inherently causal. Again like fiction, and as Debbie intuits, it is the end of the story that justifies all that precedes it. Beginnings are picked with a particular ending in mind; endings have meaning mainly as the outcome of some beginning. Consequently, the structure of the historian's argument is backward in time from the effect we know (a war, an election, or the evolution of family life) to its imputed causes (a breakdown in the political process, the emergence of new voters, a transformation in the economy). It is in this sense, too, that historical narratives are not simply descriptive, but inherently analytical. To answer the question of how or why some event, development, or process happened is to think a narrative, which is human experience (even if expressed as disembodied social forces) in some temporal sequence. Thus the process of research and analysis necessarily involves reconfiguring historical materials into a plot even if the final written product is in a nonnarrative format. It is in this sense, too, that I mean that the historian's analyses, interpretations, and explanations are all inescapably a form of narration. When historians differ over the interpretation of a historical development, therefore, they are really differing over competing historical narratives.

The fact that it is reconstructed or recovered from "traces" of human experience is another of history's crucial distinguishing features. Since historians cannot return to the present of their subjects, they cannot have complete knowledge of that past experience—just as J.J. suspects. They must rely on the "leavings"—letters, diaries, reports, maps, photographs, etc.— to reconstruct the larger story of which these artifacts were merely a part. But such leavings or traces are inert and mute; they do not become historical documents until questioned by the historian. That questioning process, or analysis, involves figuring out the context of their prior existence, the social and cultural environment of their creators, their relation to other "documents," in short, summoning the world that surrounded them. But the very fact that posing questions is the beginning point of this research process means that one must inevitably bring some of one's present to the past. This is not to say that the whole enterprise must always be presentist in perspective, but merely that a question is formulated and gains meaning only in the context of the experience of a questioner living in the present, albeit a present that includes the accumulated experience of time past.

Moreover, there is always a gap between the story accessible through the document and the story to be reconstructed. It is in this space that the historian brings to bear what one might call a disciplined creativity, or what Ricoeur calls "the subjectivity of reflection." As in fiction, both readers and creators of histories bring to bear some *a priori* notions of plausibility that shape our reactions and beliefs. We begin with what Ricoeur calls "an interpretative schemata," or historian Tom Bender, in another context, refers to as "a working image of society" already in our heads. (Ricoeur 1965; Bender 1986.) Making sense of any story, fictional as well as factual, presupposes some notions about the rules or ordering tendencies of human behavior, that is, a theory, however inchoate, of how people respond to situations and social environments. As J.J. would put it, "why ninth-grade girls storm out of houses."

Alternatively, we might think of Debbie writing about her sister. She becomes herself a primary source, but her knowledge is limited to her own observation and perspective. Her creativity comes in finding ways, and the discipline, to evoke as complete and true an image of her sister as possible. Not by *inventing* facts but by making the right choices among the facts, which involves not only her memory but her sense of what a reader is likely to respond to or be convinced by. She felt the need to include in her story more about what her family was like when her sister was well in order to show the reader the extent of their loss. Thus a working image of how humans behave, in this case how her readers will respond, is part of her analytical and creative skill.

Although historians do not have the liberty of novelists to get inside peoples' heads, they do presume—as J.J. hopes—to "talk about how they think," their motivations and purposes, much of which must be inferred rather than accessed directly. The quality and persuasiveness of the inference depends on the qualities the historian brings to bear on the problem, that is, training in the craft, experience in life, and capacity for human empathy. Of course, there is also a necessary distance between past worlds and our own, and part of the historian's discipline is to tread carefully between empathy and a respect for the otherness of past lives.

It follows from all this, I believe, that students can and ought to be taught to construct their own historical narratives. That is, taught to do in a disciplined and formal way something they already do informally and unreflectively. One does not have to wait for some moment when they have "enough" background, because whatever their background there will always be unanswered questions and gaps in their knowledge. Indeed, this is one of the things they should learn about the process and its necessary discipline. Part of the historian's skill is to recognize where the gaps are; part of the creativity is working around and through the gaps.

To enable this process, the documents we give students should not be used simply to illustrate answers already given, that is, as Debbie observes, something "that other people found out and know already." It is important, then, that the documents students work with should be genuinely open to multiple interpretations and open-ended questions. "Multiple" and "open-ended" do not mean that there are no right or wrong answers, but that "right" and "wrong" depend very much on the perspective from which a question is posed. As I hope to show below, a right answer can be incomplete; a wrong answer may still be useful in suggesting something problematic about how our present informs our view of the past. By learning to construct their own narratives, students will learn to critique others' narratives. History, then, becomes an ongoing conversation and debate rather than a dry compilation of "facts" and dates, a closed catechism, or a set of questions already answered. There is within it "a place to invent." ■

CHAPTER 3

History 413:
Making the Work of History
Visible and Open to Students

Electioneering at the South—Sketched by W.L. Sheppard.

I will try to illustrate something of what the process of teaching students to form and question historical narratives might look like by describing a moment from my own teaching experience. History 413 is a survey of the African American experience from the Civil War to the present. In the fall of 1988, I chose to emphasize the economic aspects of that experience and their consequences for race relations and ideology, culture, and social life, not only for African Americans but for the nation as a whole. This particular class enrolled 48 students, mostly juniors and seniors with a sprinkling of sophomores and graduate students; about 15 came from American minority groups, mostly African American and Asian. Although it is a single example, conducted with a college class, it shows what might be involved in making the thought behind historical narratives visible and open to a wide range of students. I am convinced, based in part on what Debbie and J.J. had to say, that even younger and less prepared students can be engaged in a more active and imaginative examination of what history offers.

The Materials of History

Any effort to teach history is shaped by the raw materials on which it draws. Consequently, it is important to look closely at the materials we typically offer beginning students—since they establish what students have in front of them. So before turning to the documents I used with my college students, let's examine excerpts about the Reconstruction period from two typical secondary school textbooks. These selections, it should be pointed out, were chosen at random and not because they are especially egregious or blameworthy examples. In fact, they might well be taken as exemplary, on the whole: accurate, fair-minded, striving for ethnic balance, and so on. They are nonetheless presentations of history Debbie would recognize: dry assemblages of fact, in which interpretation is relatively opaque.

> *The Freedmen's Bureau is established.* To help the newly freed blacks realize some of the benefits of emancipation, Congress created the Freedmen's Bureau in March, 1865.... The Freedmen's Bureau undoubtedly relieved the suffering of many Southerners displaced by the war. At times its officials were able to move people from crowded areas to other places where jobs were available. The Bureau also gave some public land to care for the ailing and aged. One of the most important contributions of the Bureau was to arrange labor contracts between black workers and their new employers (Graff 1985, 446–447).

> *Sharecropping becomes common.* Instead of selling land, many plantation owners rented their land to tenant farmers. Some tenants paid rent in cash or in crops worth the

amount of their rent. But many tenants were poor whites or blacks who could furnish nothing but their labor. They became sharecroppers. The landlord provided them with food, seed, tools, and a cabin. In return, the sharecroppers gave the landowner a share of the crops raised on their plots of land. Many sharecroppers barely made a living from their share of the crops. They were often in debt to the landowner, especially when harvests were bad. (Wilder et al. 1990, 449).

In each of these passages the dryness and blandness project a specific narrative of Reconstruction, or at least aspects of a larger implied narrative, at the same time concealing or suppressing alternative narratives. In the excerpt above from *Glorious Republic* the Freedmen's Bureau emerges as an efficient and benevolent force in the postwar adjustment process. It is not that the passage quoted is inaccurate in its facts, but the selection of facts and how they are framed tell a particular story without a hint that there might be an alternative rendition of events. Freedmen were moved from "crowded areas" to "jobs." The "giving" of public land and health care are implicitly equated by the syntax of the sentence that describes them. And among the Bureau's "most important contributions" was to arrange labor contracts between "black workers and their new employers." The text is silent on the possibility of tension between the policy choices of giving "land," moving to "jobs," and arranging "labor contracts." In fact, this passage leaves no space for questions that might challenge the imagination and test one's critical skills. How did the black ex-slaves suddenly become "workers" and the former slaveowners "new employers," one might well ask? Was this the necessary or natural outcome that should have followed emancipation? The fact that Bureau agents were required to "arrange" things suggest that it was not. What would it mean to ex-slaves to be working again for their former masters? Would they freely make that choice? What would it mean to the former masters to employ rather than own their workers? How might their attitudes affect the execution of labor contracts ?

In the passage above from *America's Story* we see the ultimate outcome of the Bureau's efforts to arrange labor contracts, the sharecropping system. But how did this become an ultimate outcome? Again, the text implies a natural process. White and African American sharecroppers were people "who could furnish nothing but their labor." Consequently, the next sentence informs us, "They became sharecroppers." Because their shares were too small and there were bad harvests, the sharecroppers fell into poverty and debt. Why this class of people would have "nothing but their labor" is not examined. How did their shares come to be too small? Why did they bear the brunt of bad harvests? This particular narrative does not suggest that such questions might even be posed. Landlessness and toollessness are merely the preexisting conditions that the planters solved by their choice to rent rather than sell their land. The croppers' shares were small because they were poor; they were poor because their shares were small.

Again the main point here is not that these narratives are necessarily inaccurate factually, but simply that they are closed, stunted versions of the history of this period. Their closure both misrepresents the dynamism of this period in "America's story" and shuts down the learning process at the very place it might begin. Indeed, something of what students are expected to "learn" from these passages is suggested by the review questions that follow at the end of their respective chapters. "What effect did the war have on the plantation system?" Wilder asks. "Why was the Freedmen's Bureau set up?" inquires Graff. Such questions cannot help but impress on students that history calls for cut-and-dried answers; that it cares mainly about austere processes and developments, about what J.J. calls "capital 'P' people" and what Debbie refers to as "someone else's facts." Most of all, students learn, history is something to be memorized rather than thought about or debated. They do not learn about what intervenes between the observed historical "facts" and textbook generalizations such as "they became sharecroppers." What intervene are analysis, interpretation, and narration, all of which are shaped by the values, skills, questions, and understandings of a particular teller.

Questions for History

Contrary to what J.J. suspects, history *is* about people, including especially the small "p" people, like the poor white and African American sharecroppers referred to in these texts. It should raise and should be the place to examine many of the fundamental, continuing questions of everyday life. The choices and struggles faced by black ex-slaves are not mere fodder for memorization, but fields of inquiry to be examined and pondered for their larger meanings for human experience.

As I prepared to teach my class about the African American experience during Reconstruction, therefore, I pondered what question would make the relevance of that experience as explicit as possible—*to this particular group of students.* Even for a class that was overwhelmingly white and middle class, the struggle for black freedom had more than historical relevance, I believed. In posing to them the question of what freedom meant for former slaves, why not first ask: "What does freedom mean to you?" I instructed them to define it not in abstract terms but in terms of their own lives.

Their answers were wide-ranging. Despite my instructions, a few gave rather pedantic answers, as if taking an exam, invoking everything from the Greeks to Karl Marx's critique of "bourgeois freedom." Others, remembering it was a history course after all, invoked the Constitution and Bill of Rights: free speech, assembly, religion, and so forth. But several answered in terms of the mundane features of everyday life. For example, one young woman thought of being finally free of parental oversight and able to stay out late. Another, recently from a Catholic high school, savored the right *not* to have to wear uniforms. A feminist activist mentioned freedom of reproductive rights and from violence to her person. Running through all, of course, was the notion of "choice," of self-determination, and autonomy; but these were words extracted from the discussion that ensued. This group thought in terms of what late nineteenth-century liberals called "negative freedom" rather than "positive freedom," i.e., freedom from restraint rather than the possession of the resources necessary for self-realization. Only five of the 41 respondents added access to resources— material, educational, health, etc.—as essential components of freedom. For the most part they were closer to John Stuart Mill's *On Liberty* than to Franklin Delano Roosevelt's "Four Freedoms." Nonetheless, their answers provided a place from which to open our discussion of Reconstruction.

Following this exercise, we turned to a discussion of a selection of documents, all drawn from a documentary collection of Civil War and post–Civil War letters, reports, and other sources (Berlin et al. 1986). Fresh from having posed the question of the meaning of freedom in their own lives, they were now asked to pose that same question for African Americans just emerging from slavery in 1865. First they were asked to "deconstruct" the Emancipation Proclamation by asking these questions: What were its terms? What were its limitations? What do you imagine its impact was in the context of a revolutionary conflict? Next they examined a long letter from a slaveholder to the Confederate President, surprisingly, supporting a Confederate emancipation measure, but a measure structured so as to maintain control over black laborers by depriving them of any alternative employment to working on the same plantations they had worked on as slaves.

For the next day's discussion, they were presented a second set of documents clustered around a particular set of closely spaced events in such a way as to help them grasp the narrative aspect of history. The first was a letter written by freedmen stating in their own terms precisely what they expected freedom to mean. The second was written by a Freedmen's Bureau agent, almost as if in reply to the first (though it was not), and represents the view of many northerners committed to the ideology of free wage labor, or at least one variant of it. The final document was a report on the views of an African American Bureau agent who articulated a more radical view of what freedom requires. Each of these documents, as part of this larger whole, was also chosen to help students understand one moment in history as the interplay of many lines of action, conflicting desires, and dramatically different conceptions of what freedom should bring.

Having worked with these and similar documents, I entered the class with a number of preconceptions about their meaning and the narrative I expected students to extract from or construct about emancipation's aftermath. But materials like these are "live," that is, they allow the students direct access to see and hear for themselves and thus to formulate their own questions and answers. Such questions arise in the space between the document itself and the reader's experience, what he or she *brings to* the material. Consequently, one should not be surprised when they do find new and unexpected meanings or raise fresh questions that are sometimes not immediately answerable. In fact, the most successful discussions are neither predictable, controllable, nor closable. And that is as it should be.

Interpreting the Simple Facts: The Letter from Edisto Island

During his famous "March to the Sea" from Atlanta to the South Carolina coast, General William T. Sherman found his army inundated with tens of thousands of former slave refugees who followed in the army's track. At the suggestion of a group of African American leaders and in response to the federal government's anxiety to address the more general problem of what to do with freed slaves, Sherman issued a military order in January 1865 that allocated thousands of acres of abandoned islands along the Atlantic coast from South Carolina to northern Florida in 40-acre plots to African American families. The Lincoln administration made a firm commitment to seek legislation during the ensuing Congressional session making freedmen's titles to the land permanent. But in October 1865 President Andrew Johnson, pursuing a policy of reconciling the white South, pardoned former rebels and restored their property. This meant that the freedmen had to accept eviction or agree to work the land under the former slaveowners for wages. It was the first of a series of steps that squashed any hope of

The Letter from Edisto Island

[Edisto Island, S.C. October 28?, 1865]

General—It Is with painful Hearts that we the Committe address you, we Have thurougholy considerd the order which you wished us to Signn, we wish we could <u>do</u> so but cannot feel our rights Safe If we do so,

General we want Homesteads; we were promised Homesteads by the government; If It does not carry out the promises Its agents made to us, If the government Haveing concluded to befriend Its late enemies and to neglect to observe the principles of common faith between Its self and us Its allies In the war you said was over, now takes away from them all right to the soil they stand upon save such as they can get by again working for <u>your</u> late and their <u>alltime</u> <u>enemies.</u>—If the government does so

we are left in a more unpleasant condition than our former we are at the mercy of those who are combined to prevent us from getting land enough to lay our Fathers bones upon. We Have property In Horses, cattle, carriages, & articles of furniture, but we are landless and Homeless, from the Homes we have lived In In the past we can only do one of three things

Step Into the public <u>road or the sea</u> or remain on them working as In former time and subject to their will as then. We can not resist It In any way without being driven out Homeless upon the road.

You will see this Is not the condition of really freemen

You ask us to forgive the land owners of our Island. <u>You</u> only lost your right arm. In war and might forgive them.

significant land reform in the South, thereby limiting the possible meanings freedom might come to have for black Americans. General O. O. Howard, who was generally sympathetic to the freedmen's aspirations, journeyed to Edisto Island off the coast of South Carolina personally to inform a church filled with ex-slaves that the land was no longer theirs. The government's promise would not be honored. In shock and disbelief the freedpeople drafted a plea to Howard asking that this

The man who tied me to a tree & gave me 39 lashes & who stripped and flogged my mother & sister & who will not let me stay In His empty Hut except I will do His planting & be Satisfied with His price & who combines with others to keep away land from me well knowing I would not Have any thing to do with Him If I Had land of my own. — that man, I cannot well forgive. Does It look as if He Has forgiven me, seeing How He tries to keep me In a Condition of Helplessness

General, we cannot remain Here In such condition and If the government permits them to come back we ask It to Help us to reach land where we shall not be slaves nor compelled to work for those who would treat us as such

we Have not been treacherous, we Have not for selfish motives allied to us those who suffered like us from a common enemy & then Haveing gained <u>our</u> purpose left our allies In thier Hands   There is no rights secured to us there Is no law likely to be made which our Hands can reach. The state will make laws that we shall not be able to Hold land even If we pay for It   Landless, Homeless, Voteless, we can only pray to god & Hope for <u>His Help, your Influence & assistance</u>   With consideration of esteem Your Obt Servts

In behalf of the people

Henry Bram

Committee Ishmael WIoultrie

yates Sampson

Ira Berlin, Steven Hahn, Steven F. Miller, Joseph P. Reidy, Leslie S. Rowland. "The Terrain of Freedom: The Struggle over the Meaning of Free Labor in the U.S. South," <u>History Workshop.</u> Autumn 1986. pp. 127-28.

fateful decision be reconsidered (see The Letter from Edisto Island).

My intent in using this document was framed by my own initial reaction upon first reading it some years ago. What I was struck by first was the clarity as well as poignancy of the freedmen's idea of what their liberation from slavery should mean in both material and social terms. Indeed, this brief document contains a rich repository of material from which a provisional narrative of both slavery and emancipation could be constructed, *from the freedmen's perspective.* What was their experience under slavery like, or at least what do they recall as most important about that experience? That is, what might their first-person narrative look like? What do they seem to value? In other words, exactly what do land, family, elders, loyalty, and honor mean to them? What is their apparent understanding of their relation to the state— federal and local—and to politics ("Landless, Homeless, Voteless")?

My students were prepared to empathize fully with the Edisto petitioners. The freedmen's sense of betrayal is palpable and unimpeachable. They also could see the petitioner's crucial point that material resources, in this case land, were essential preconditions for exercising genuine self-determination or self-realization in the postwar South. They shared their anxiety that the "freedom" merely to work for those who had formerly enslaved them was suspect. No one raised the contrary argument—popular among many conservative and liberal northerners at the time and some later historians of the period as well— that no one is entitled to receive land or property they have not earned by savings from their own labor. Had they done so, it might have provided an opportunity to explore more fully the freedmen's idea that they had *already* earned a right to the land, by their work and suffering as slaves ("tied me to a tree & gave me 39 lashes & who stripped and flogged my mother & sister & who will not let me stay In His empty Hut"). Clearly the land has come to mean more than a means of material support; it is a place to bury their "Fathers bones upon."

It quickly became apparent that pursuing some of these questions called for research into other sources and documents. What was the political situation in South Carolina that the petitioners make oblique reference to when they say "the state will make laws"? Who is this General Howard, the emissary of bad news, whom they feel free to address in trustful but reproachful tones ("You only lost your right arm")? Posing questions that cannot be answered solely from the information supplied by the document itself and requiring students to undertake additional research was an important lesson to students about the task the historian faces. In my class student volunteers were asked to look up specific factual matters before the day of the discussion and to contribute their findings at the appropriate juncture. In some cases they identified people involved (like General Howard) or policies (Sherman's Field Order No. 15) or filled in unfamiliar background (like black military service during the war).

But I realized again in listening to my students' information that the process of interpretation cannot be reduced to simply a matter of accumulating facts. The facts will not simply speak for themselves. The facts chosen for inclusion, the order of their presentation, the point of view adopted (Howard's? the Edisto freedmen?)—all make for a profoundly different story. Beginning not with the eviction order but with the freedmen's memory of slavery and their resultant sense of entitlement makes for a radically different narrative. Moreover, in the unfilled "spaces" between the facts there is room for imaginative reconstruction or inference from the known to the possible; or "to make it up," as J.J. would say. For example, the freedmen declare that they have property: "Horses, cattle, carriages, & articles of furniture"; such a statement might be a stimulus for more research into the conditions of slavery. But it could also provide an occasion for reflection and imaginative reconstruction. People who legally belonged to others—the lowliest status possible in a free society—also owned property, valued and nurtured kinship ties, and aspired to landownership. What might all this imply about the larger political situation in the South? From this letter alone it is apparent that freedmen were capable of organizing collectively to petition the highest authorities in the land to redress their grievances. They were capable as a community of defining and articulating what is politically right and morally just. Contrary to the opinions of many of their white contemporaries and not a few historians since, such a people were "ready" for freedom. What might that "freedom" have looked like had government policies been different? Had the Bureau's efforts "to arrange labor contracts" *not* been its "most important contribution"? Had the sharecroppers, white and black, not been landless and toolless?

Soule's Letter

To the Freed People of Orangeburg District.

You have heard many stories about your condition as freemen. You do not know what to believe: you are talking too much; waiting too much; asking for too much. If you can find out the truth about this matter, you will settle down quietly to your work. Listen, then, and try to understand just how you are situated.

You are now free, but you must know that the only difference you can feel yet, between slavery and freedom, is that neither you nor your children can be bought or sold. You may have a harder time this year than you have ever had before; it will be the price you pay for your freedom. You will have to work hard, and get very little to eat, and very few clothes to wear. If you get through this year alive and well, you should be thankful. Do not expect to save up anything, or to have much corn or provisions ahead at the end of the year. You must not ask for more pay than free people get at the North. There, a field hand is paid in money, but has to spend all his pay every week, in buying food and clothes for his family and in paying rent for his house. You cannot be paid in money,—for there is no good money in the District,—nothing but Confederate paper. Then, what can you be paid with? Why, with food, with clothes, with the free use of your little houses and lots. You do not own a cent's worth except yourselves. The plantation you live on is not yours, not the houses, nor the cattle, mules and horses; the seed you planted with was not yours, and the ploughs and hoes do not belong to you. Now you must get something to eat and something to wear, and houses to live in. How can you get these things? By hard work—nothing else, and it will be a good thing for you if you get them until next year, for yourselves and for your families. You must remember that your children, your old people, and the cripples, be-long to you to support now, and all that is given to them is so much pay to you for your work. If you ask for anything more; if you ask for a half of the crop, or even a third, you ask too much; you wish to get more than you could get if you had been free all your lives.... Do not think, because you are free you can chose your own kind of work. Every man must work under orders. The soldiers, who are free, work under officers, the officers under the general, and the general under the president. There must be a head man everywhere, and on a plantation the head man, who gives all the orders, is the owner of the place. Whatever he tells you to do you must do at once, and cheerfully. Never give him a cross word or an impudent answer....

There are different kinds of work. One man is a doctor, another is a minister, another a soldier. One black man may be a field hand, one a blacksmith, one a carpenter, and still another a house-servant. Every man has his own place, his own trade that he was brought up to, and he must stick to it. The house-servants must not want to go into the field, nor the field hands into the house. If a man works, no matter in what business, he is doing well. The only shame is to be idle and lazy.

You do not understand why some of the white people who used to own you, do not have to work in the field. It is because they are rich. If every man were poor, and worked in his own field, there would be no big farms, and very little cotton or corn raised to sell; there would be no money, and nothing to buy. Some people must be rich, to pay the others, and they have the right to do no work except to look out after their property. It is so everywhere, and perhaps by hard work some of you may by-and-by become rich yourselves.

Remember that all your working time belongs to the man who hires you: therefore you must not leave work without his leave not even to nurse a child, or to go and visit a wife or husband. When you wish to go off the place, get a pass as you used to, and then you will run no danger of being taken up by our soldiers. If you leave work for a day, or if you are sick, you cannot expect to be paid for what you do not do, and the man who hires you must pay less at the end of the year.

Do not think of leaving the plantation where you belong. If you try to go to Charleston, or any other city, you will find no work to do, and nothing to eat. You will starve, or fall sick and die. Stay where you are, in your own homes, even if you are suffering. There is no better place for you anywhere else.

You will want to know what to do when a husband and wife live on different places. Of course they ought to be together, but this year, they have their crops planted in their own places, and they must stay to work them. At the end of the year they can live to-gether. Until then, they must see each other only once in a while.

In every set of men there are some bad men and some fools; who have to be looked after and punished when they go wrong. The Government will punish grown people now, and punish them severely, if they steal, lie idle, or hang around a man's place when he does not want them there, or if they are impudent. You ought to be civil to one another, and to the man you work for. Watch folks that have always been free, and you will see that the best people are the most civil.

The children have to be punished more than those who are grown up, for they are full of mischief. Fathers and mothers should punish their own children, but if they happen to be off, or if the child is caught stealing or behaving badly about the big house, the owner of the plantation must switch him, just as he should his own children.

Do not grumble if you cannot get as much pay on your place as some one else, for on one place they have more children than on others, on one place the land is poor, on another it is rich; on one place Sherman took everything, on another, perhaps, almost everything was left safe. One man can afford to pay more than another. Do not grumble, either, because the meat is gone or the salt is hard to get. Make the best of everything, and if there is anything you think is wrong, or hard to bear, try to reason it out: if you cannot, ask leave to send one man to town to see an officer. Never stop work on any account, for the whole crop must be raised and got in, or we shall starve. The old men, and the men who mean to do right, must agree to keep order on every plantation. When they see a hand getting lazy or shiftless, they must talk to him, and if talk will do no good, they must take him to the owner of the plantation.

In short, do just about what the good men among you have always done. Remember that even if you are badly off, no one can buy or sell you: remember that if you help yourselves, *God* will help you, and trust hopefully that next year and the year after will bring some new blessing to you.

The Question of Values: Captain Soule's Letter

Questions such as those above are more likely to develop as the examination moves through several related and contrastive documents rather than in the discussion of a single piece. In the preceding letter, Captain Charles C. Soule, a white Union officer who served with the Freedmen's Bureau in coastal South Carolina, makes the case *against* black landownership and *for* wage labor. Like many other northerners, Soule was more concerned with sustaining the southern economy through the production of cotton and other staples than with the welfare of blacks. Or more accurately, he was convinced that the latter could only be achieved through the former policy in any case. Ex-slaves would be fitted for freedom through the discipline of wage labor. Those who adapted best to that discipline would naturally find opportunities to make their way up the agricultural ladder and become farm owners themselves. Only a few could expect to be that lucky, however; most would have to settle for the lowly but honorable subordination and dependence of working for others all their lives. The letter is a speech to freedmen that Soule had recorded and reported to his superiors.

What is fascinating about students' responses to the Soule document is that although they found him distasteful, they could not completely dissociate themselves from the notion of economic justice and order that he describes. After all, they are themselves creatures of a wage-labor economy. In that light, the freedmen's vision of a society of independent farmers and craftsmen is but a fond, nostalgic memory. With subtle prodding I could return them to our earlier discussions of freedom and ask them to reexamine their earlier definitions of freedom. How is their world different from the freedmen's that they can feel free yet not own farms, shops, or the tools of their trade? Or is it different at all? One student, J.B. (who had earlier defined freedom as simply the right to say "No"), angered everyone by declaring bluntly that Soule was right. "Everyone has to work for someone else or starve. That's just the way it is!" Most saw a blatant contradiction in a society that extolled the inherent value of labor, yet exempted those with property from that requirement. And Soule's insistence that the propertyless should support the system because otherwise there would be no one to pay wages brought guffaws. My class was convinced that the freedmen of Edisto seemed perfectly capable of self-support had they been given the means to make a start.

Nonetheless, we left hanging the deeper question raised by J.B.'s rude challenge: If the freedmen were being deprived of

A Report on Major Delany

Beaufort, S.C., July 24th 1865.

[to Brev. Maj. S.M. Taylor] Major In obedience to your request, I proceeded to St Helena Island, yesterday morning, for the purpose of listening to the public delivery of a lecture by Major Delany 104th U.S. Col. Troops

I was accompanied by Lieut A Whyte jr 128th U.S.C.T., under orders of Col C.H. Howard 128th U.S.C.T. Comd'g Post.

The meeting was held near "Brick Church," the congregation numbering from 500 to 600.

As introduction Maj Delaney, made them acquainted with the fact that slavery is absolutely abolished, throwing thunders of damnations and maledictions on all the former Slaveowners and People of the South, and almost condemned their souls to hell.

He says "It was only a War policy of the Government, to declare the slaves of the South free, knowing that the whole power of the South laid in the possession of Slaves.

"But I want you to <u>understand</u> that we would not have become free, had we not armed ourselves and fought out our independence" (this he repeated twice)

He farther says "If I had been a slave, I would have been most troublesome and not to be conquered by any threat or punishment. I would not have worked, and no one would have dared to come near me, I would have struggled for life or death, and would have thrown fire and sword between them. I know <u>you</u> have been good, only too good.

I was told by a friend of mine; that when owned by a man and put to work on the field, he laid quietly down, and just looked out for the overseer to come along, when he pretended to work very hard. But he confessed to me, that he never has done a fair days work for his master. And so he was right, so I would have done the same, and all of you ought to have done the same.

People say that you are too lazy to work, that you have not the intelligence to get on for yourselves without being guided and driven to the work by overseers. I say it is a lie, and a blasphemous lie, and I will prove it to be so.

Your masters who lived in opulence, kept you to hard work, by some most contemptible being—called overseer—who chastised and

THINKING HISTORICALLY

beat you whenever he pleased—while your master lived in Northern town or in Europe to squander away the wealth only you acquired for him. He never earned a single Dollar in his life. You men and women, every one of you around me, made thousands and thousands of dollars. Only you were the means for your masters to lead the idle and inglorious life, and to give his children the education, which he denied you, for fear you may awake to conscience. If I look around me, I tell you, all the houses on this Island and in Beaufort, they are all familiar to my eye, they are the same structures which I have met with in Africa. They have all been made by the Negroes, you can see it by their rude exterior. I tell you they (White man) cannot teach you anything, and they could not make them because they have not the brain to do it. (After a pause) At least I mean the Southern people; "Oh the Yankees they are smart." Now tell me from all you have heard from me, are you not worth anything? Are you those men whom they think, God only created as a curse and for a slave? Whom they do not consider their equals? As I said before the Yankees are smart—there are good ones and bad ones. The good ones, if they are good they are very good, if they are bad, they are very bad. But the worst and most contemptible, and even worse than even your masters were, are those Yankees, who hired themselves as overseers—

Believe not in these School teachers, Emissaries Ministers and agents, because they never tell you the truth, and I particularly warn you against those Cotton Agents, who come honey mouthed unto you, their only intent being to make profit by your inexperience.

If there is a man comes to you, who will meddle with your affairs, send him to one of your more enlightened brothers, who shall ask him, who he is, what business he seeks with you etc.

Believe none but those Agents who are sent out by the Government, to enlighten and guide you.

Now I will come to the main purpose for which I have come to see you. As before the whole South depended upon you, now the whole country will depend upon you. I give you an advice how to get along. Get up a community and get all the lands you can—if you cannot get any singly. Grow as much vegetables etc. as you want for your families; on the other part of land you cultivate Rice and Cotton.... Now you understand that I want you to be producers of this country. It is the wish of the Government for you to be so. We will send friends to you, who will further instruct you how to come to the end of our wishes. You see that by so adhering to our views, you will become a wealthy and powerful population.

Now I look around me and I notice a man, bare footed covered with rags and dirt. Now I ask, what is that man doing, for whom is he working. I hear that he works for that and that farmer "for 30 cents a day". "I tell you that must not be." "That would be cursed slavery over again." "I will not have it, the Government will not have it, and the Government shall hear about it, I will tell the Government.

I tell you slavery is over, and shall never return again. We have now 200,000 of our men well drilled in arms and used to War fare, and I tell you it is with you and them that slavery shall not come back again, and if you are determined it will not return again.

Now go to work, and in a short time I will see you again, and other friends will come to show you how to begin.

Have your fields in good order and well tilled and well planted, and when I pass the fields and see a land well planted and well cared for, then I may be sure from the look of it that it belongs to a free negroe, and when I see a field thinly planted and little cared for, then I may think it belongs to some man who works it with slaves. The Government decided that you should have one third of the produce of the crops from your employer, so if he makes $3-, you will have to get $1- out of it for your labour. The other day some plantation owners in Virginia and Maryland offered $5.- a month for your labour, but it was indignantly rejected by Genl Howard, the Commissioner for the Government.

These are the expressions, as far as I can remember, without having made notice at the time.

The excitement with the congregation was immense, groups were formed talking over, what they heard, and ever and anon cheers were given to some particular sentences of the speech.

I afterwards mingled with several groups, to hear their opinions. Some used violent language, "saying they would get rid of the Yankee employer."—"That is the only man who ever told them the truth." "That now those men have to work themselves or starve or leave the country, we will not work for them anymore."

Some Whites were present, and listened with horror depicted in their faces, to the whole performance. Some said "What shall become of us now? and if such a speech should again be given to those men, there will be open rebellion...

My opinion of the whole affair is, that Major Delany is a thorough hater of the White race, and tries the colored people unnecessarily. He even tries to injure the magnanimous conduct of the Government towards them, either intentionally or through want of knowledge. He tells them to remember, "that they would not have become free, had they not armed themselves and fought for their independence. This is a falsehood and a misrepresentation. — Our President Abraham Lincoln declared the Colored race free, before there was even an idea of arming colored men. This ids decidedly calculated to create bad feelings against the Government.

By giving some historical facts and telling them that neither Indians nor whites could stand the work in the country, he wants to impress the colored man with the idea, that he is in fact superior not only in a physical view but als(o) in intelligence. He says "believe none of the ministers, Schoolteachers, Emissaries, because they never tell you the truth." It is only to bring distrust against all, and gives them to understand, that they shall believe men of their own race. He openly acts and speaks contrary to the policy of this Government, advising them not to work for any man, but for themselves.

The intention of our Government is, that all the men shall be employed by their former masters as far as possible, and contracts made between them, superintended by some officer empowered by the Government.

He says it would be the old slavery over again. If a man should work for an employer, and that it must not be. Does he not give a hint of what they shall do, by his utterings "that if he had been a slave etc?; or by giving the narrative of the slave who did not work for his master? — further as he says: that a field should show by its appearance by whom and for whom it is worked?

The mention of having two hundred thousand men well drilled in arms: — does he not hint to them what to do? — if they should be compelled to work for employers?

In my opinion by this discourse he was trying to encourage them, to break the peace of society and force their way by insurrection to a position he is ambitious they should attain to. I am, Major, Very Respectfully Your obedt servant

Edward M. Stoeber

real freedom, what about us? In this particular class I hoped to let that question simmer, returning to it in a slightly different context later in the course. It is, however, one that might stimulate an extended, more engaged discussion than students might be accustomed to in history classes. It is an open-ended question; that is, there is no right or final answer. Indeed some may attack the validity of the question itself. Is it framed so as to presuppose that something is wrong or inadequate about the American ideal of freedom and economic opportunity? But if nothing is wrong, was the treatment of the freedmen unjust? The teacher, like the students, will bring to this discussion perspectives, political views and values, anxieties and predispositions that overdetermine their answers. But as such, these are the kind of questions that expose the "knowledge" we all bring to any act of historical interpretation. The act of interpretation cannot be value neutral or entirely objective. The "discipline" we aspire to is to bring the values and subjective influences out into the open. In other words, we must ask questions of ourselves as well as of the documents.

Interrogating the Evidence: A Report on Major Delany

Another kind of discipline we seek to develop as historians is learning how to ask the right questions of our documents. Not only what do they tell us but also can we trust what they tell us? J.J.'s question.

One of Captain Soule's fellow Bureau agents, Edward M. Stoeber, filed the report (reprinted on pages 32–34) on the activities of another officer, Major Martin R. Delany. Of northern free African American parentage, Delany had already had a rich and distinguished career before working as a Bureau agent in South Carolina. He had edited a newspaper with Frederick Douglass, attended Harvard to work on a degree in medicine, written several books and pamphlets advocating black nationalism, worked in the abolitionist movement, and traveled widely in Africa and Europe. More recently he had recruited, organized, and commanded black soldiers for the Union Army, eventually becoming one of only two African Americans to attain the field grade rank of major. Ten years later Delany would be an unsuccessful candidate for lieutenant governor of South Carolina.

My students immediately hit upon the key question one must ask about this document: How much can it be trusted as an accurate record of the events at Brick Church? How much as a characterization of Martin Delany's views or intent? Professional historians bring to their interpretation of documents varying degrees of background knowledge about its larger context and the people who produce it or who are implicated in it. Thus my students' relative ignorance about Reconstruction, federal policy toward freedmen, African American contributions to the Union's victory in the Civil War, or Martin Delany's activities before and after 1865 differs in degree from the professional's—but not in kind. These are all questions that can stimulate additional research. Learning to recognize and pose them is part of the process of learning about history. It is about questions as well as answers.

But a close reading of the text can produce answers and insights quite apart from the questions it raises. Something of the character of Stoeber, of Delany, and of the freed people emerges, despite our wariness of the accuracy of this report. The tension between Delany's policy views and Stoeber's is transparent: They advocate very different futures for the freedmen. Stoeber's pseudo-verbatim recounting (he admits that he did not take notes at the meeting) in the body of the report contrasts sharply with his characterization at the end. Reading the words attributed to Delany, my students did not conclude that he was fomenting insurrection or counseling the freedmen not to work or even that they not work for whites. Indeed, he urged them to work diligently and aspire to buy farms of their own. It was his insistence that they not work for "slave-like" wages that upset Stoeber and the white employers in attendance. From this single document, then, the larger outline of the contemporaneous conflict, between the aspirations of freedmen, planters, and the federal government, emerges. When considered along with the earlier documents, a broader discussion is possible not only about the constraints on black freedom following slavery but also about competing notions regarding the meaning and substance of freedom still relevant to our own lives. Through interrogating such documents, then, one achieves the difficult balance of making history immediate, of understanding it in the terms of its historical personalities and times, at the same time making it relevant to and alive in our own time.

But the use of documents need not be confined to classroom discussions like those described here. Throughout History 413 I tried to unfold for my students the process of thinking historically with the hope that they would eventually take that process on. For me, midterms and finals were not tests in the traditional sense. Rather, they were occasions for students to perform as historians. I was much less interested in recognition knowledge than in what they could *do* as historians. On their take-home midterm examination, for example, I gave my students three labor contracts from different periods and asked them to act as curators preparing an annotation of the documents to accompany a display in a museum. Students were evaluated on how much information they could extract from the documents and on their skill in elaborating the historical context concisely and accurately. On their in-class final, I gave students much shorter excerpts from a variety of documents and asked them to draw on their knowledge of the relevant history and a close reading of the text to reconstruct the larger narrative of which the document was part.

The ultimate goal, however, was not to make every member of History 413 a historian, but to inculcate perspectives and develop skills that would make them better consumers of the histories written by others. The histories they read, after all, went through a similar process of analysis and interpretation of documents much like those they had examined. From their own experience working with such documents, it is hoped, they will be prepared to be active rather than passive readers of historical narratives, thinking about what is not in the historians' texts and how what is there got there. In the end, perhaps they will be not only better students of history, but better, more critical thinkers and citizens. ■

CHAPTER 4

High School Students as Historians: What Resources Do They Have?

The Separation of the Mother and Child

T he professional historian is trained to build a historical narrative from traces and leavings by applying disciplined intuition and analysis. I would argue that high school students could and should do the same. The interviews with Debbie and J.J. hint that students understand a good deal—perhaps much more than we ever suspected—about the workings of narrative and the questions we should bring to our own and others' analyses. These are an indispensable beginning; we ought to build on such prior understandings.

Yet many people would say that shaping a piece of autobiography or fiction is nothing like what a historian does; the rules of evidence, the search for and the verification of sources, the gradual synthesis of different lines of information, the generation of a thesis—where are these? Students often claim, with J.J., that history won't take us inside the mind of a young girl in Kirkwood, Missouri, so what good is it? Can we expect students to use what they know about personal, autobiographical narrative in learning to write history? Can they imagine the kinds of narratives that will let them find not just *their* lives, but also lives of different times and places, in a journal, a will, or a treaty? Can they sense what is lost or skewed or partial? Can they think of history as being about competing narratives? If they do so, can they see the deep-running human issues being debated in those different narratives?

These are the questions that matter. But not questions to be answered in the abstract. Again, it is important to put students in situations that will let them answer fully and then to listen quite carefully to what they have to say. To this end, the documents from History 413 were given to a high school history class that was asked to read and talk about them—once quite early in its study of American History and again when the class had had some chance to think about the way history works. What follows is an account of one student's confrontation with those documents, particularly the letter from Edisto Island. In it we ask: "Can students enter the worlds suggested by historical documents?" "Can they understand history as conflicting narratives?" "Can they formulate historical questions leading to their own narratives?" "Can they fill out these questions with information and analysis?" "Can they grapple with the questions of value in history?"

Entering a Document: A High School Student Reads the Letter from Edisto Island

Zev is 16. He is a white student in a school that is struggling to understand what it means to be a multi-cultural institution, not just in a decorative sense: a course in Latin American history or Zora Neale Hurston on the reading list; but by struggling day in, day out, deeply and fairly. Zev has access to, is not alienated from, American culture: The novels of his people are taught, their history is the history required for all eleventh graders across the state. But his is the "other side" of the necessity for multi-cultural education. Only if he has the chance to be a stranger, i.e., to read an American history that includes other groups as more than illustrations or to make his way through a tale where the imagery isn't his by reflex, will his education be anything more than a narrow rehearsal of the familiar.

Zev is a beginner at American history. What he knows about the Civil War and Reconstruction is slight, mythic, only hearsay: wicked plantation owners, illiterate and cowed slaves, tall Lincoln in a stovepipe hat. Even so, we asked him to read the letter from Edisto Island and to talk aloud about what he found there. At first, he felt uncomfortable, even unwilling, to "imagine his way into" the letter from Edisto Island. His notion of history was reminiscent of Debbie's: to do history is to marshall the facts, not to "guess" or deal in "stories":

> *Zev:* Come on, that's not fair. I don't know anything about the Civil War, or what happened after. It's stupid for me to be guessing about it. You can't just read into a document like it's some kind of story that ends any way you want it. It's cheating, changing the record.

But as Zev reads the letter, it provokes a series of narratives. Zev thinks—has always thought until now—of slaves as illiterates and without resources. So the letter puzzles him, and he has to imagine how it came to be:

> *Zev:* Are these spellings meant to be like this? I guess it's written the way it was written.... I would bet there were white people, underground railroad people, who worked on that letter.

> *Interviewer:* Why?

> *Zev:* I am sure that they drafted a letter and then they had someone who was working with them who was able to take out most, to take out a good number of the misspelled, wrongly stated phrases. I don't want to sound like they couldn't do it, I mean, these were smart people. It's just . . .

it seems so English, fancy writing. Let me read this sentence to you: "Consideration of your obt. servants."

The confrontation is fierce as the old, familiar narrative clashes with a newer one suggested by the powerful feelings and poignant phrases of the Edisto Island letter. Zev pauses often and struggles to find the right words; he doesn't want to sound prejudiced, but how could this letter have come about? As part of trying to understand, Zev is drawn into alliance with the writers. He slips into an almost dramatic mode, sometimes taking the stance of an observer, sometimes speaking as if he were a participant. With that, he sees the freedpeople's problem not as writing and spelling, but as having to find a way to speak to people who are unlikely to listen.

Zev: What else can you do? You know everything is taken away, you have nothing. What gets me is that last sentence: "The state will make laws that we shall not be able to hold land even if we pay for it. Landless, homeless, voteless, we can only pray to God and hope for his help." So they say to themselves, "Look, we need to get these guys as close to their game as we can. We've got one not very good shot left." And when you have one not very good shot, you gotta make it as good as you can. I mean if they go out there and get mad, they are dumb blacks, they don't understand, they are just dumb, poor, uneducated. The only thing they can hope for is for someone, like Lincoln, to step in and do something. By using a letter that shows that they are thoughtful human beings who are being taken advantage of...

But in order to enter those lives, Zev has to imagine a sequence of events that led up to the letter:

Zev: It's not a reactionary [sic] letter. If this was their first reaction, there would be a whole lot of four letter words in it. It's been thought out. There's been the reactionary stage where everyone has cussed and been mad and sad and crying and angry. And now the only thing they can hope to do is play the white man's game . . . which is to put your document against their document. Maybe they formed a committee, and then they figured out, "Look, all of us going on like this isn't going to help, we need to find the people who can do it."

But the events will not fill out unpeopled. Zev has to ask, "Who, among freedpeople, could write this letter?"

> *Zev:* They are people who are very much trying to present themselves as educated, white . . . I mean, they aren't trying to be someone else, but they have to win on their [whites'] grounds. So [it was] probably the ones who could read and write. The people who had been able to get an education. So the others say, "We'll support you; you're the ones who know, so you help us."

But as he casts the scene, Zev realizes something about the "threeness" of the men he imagines crowded around a table to draft, redraft, and then sign the letter.

> *Zev:* I can imagine one of them being very angry and another one of them saying, "Look, you be as angry as you want, that isn't going to help us." Just listen [reads from letter]: "We have not been treacherous, we have not for selfish motives allied to us those who suffered like us from a common enemy." That's not the words of an angry person. That's the words of a thoughtful, careful person who has been wronged.

The threesome evokes a connection between Edisto Island and the world Zev knows at present:

> *Zev:* They were all the ones who broke the barriers of reading and writing, but you could be looking at one Martin Luther King and one Malcolm X. Or you could look at Jesse Jackson. There are three men here; those are three men who broke the barrier together, but all three could go their separate ways.

Having connected past with present, Zev realizes there are things he can't know about a world so far away in time and place, even though he is bound to wonder about them:

> *Zev:* Were they holding in so much that it made them sick just to write? Was it, "You killers, for taking my land," or was it, "Look, this is what we got to do"? You know, this

letter is a lead pipe mask; I mean this letter is a mask so deep you can just never see through it. "Because this is our only shot at this" is all I can get from it. But I want to know what came out before the pen went to the paper. What was the first five minutes of that discussion? What's in the ashes that are now on that church floor?

Having imagined the rage and determination and the triangle of opinions around the table, Zev is not limited to imagining the concrete details of who said what. If he is asked, Zev can turn to the large and difficult question of freedom and particularly how differently different people define it—the issue at the heart of the documents from History 413:

> *Interviewer:* What do these three men think freedom is?
>
> *Zev:* Something that is a long way off. What freedom is . . . [long pause as he returns to letter]. " . . . you ask us to forgive the landowners of our island. You only lost your right arm. The man who tied me to a tree & gave me 39 lashes & who stripped and flogged my mother & sister & who will not let me stay In His empty Hut": Freedom means never having to think of a life like that, a life without fear of that. A life empty of that kind of helplessness, of no justice, of no system to protect you. [Another long pause while he thinks.] But if you don't have land, if you don't own it, you're having to rent it back all the time. You're just slaves under a different name. The laws and the promises are no good to you. It's just the same argument as is going on today—that blacks have the same opportunities. It is truer now, but not true. I mean to say, I am trying to come to modern day because it is the only thing I can talk from. People say blacks can go to their neighborhood schools; they can live in housing projects. Hey, a housing project has a bed. Of course, you have to walk in that door every night and not be shot by a drug dealer. It's the same, on the surface, you have the same rights. Just no way to get them.

This is an interview, not a short exchange in the midst of classroom conversation; it spreads out over 20 uninterrupted minutes. There is time for Zev to resist and then get caught up in meeting head-on what is new in the moving, puzzling document that lies on the table in front of him. Classrooms of 25 students rarely afford the time that Zev got. Still Zev and what he says should be taken seriously. First, he would never have wrestled with his unexamined narrative about slaves as illiterate and helpless if he hadn't met up with the people from Edisto Island—through the letter they left behind. It speaks to him at a level he believes: Its words and phrases, puzzling as they are, convey the authority of a genuine, compelling experience. College is too late to come face to face with such documents. Expanded beyond treaties and proclamations to include journals, letters, and eyewitness accounts, primary documents endow history with texture and force.

Zev says, just as Debbie and J.J. did, that students feel this force. They can give credence to other people's experience; they can give meaning to the past by examining it in the light of what their empathy and their knowledge of their own immediate world offers. They can discover the contours of other human lives in the traces those lives have left—uncovering, in the process, a history that calls for analysis, but insists on imagination.

Reading Conflicting Narratives

Yet history isn't one univocal force. There is a different story of Reconstruction in Soule's letter, in the report on Delany, and in the freedpeople's letter. What are the chances that beginning students can grasp history as an argument among competing narratives? Must they be presented with just one, uncontested narrative?

I think not. Zev's teacher begins his class by taking the sturdiest myths of American growing-up—Columbus discovering America, Lincoln freeing the slaves—and asks his students, from the outset, to learn that there isn't simply one correct rendition of history.

Zev: Mr. J. is very interested in showing us points of view that you've absolutely never seen and never been told. Last night we read two things. One was Kelly, our textbook, the part about "The Beginning of Slavery." Then we read a Xerox history by Lerone Bennett, called *Before the Mayflower*.

When I read the Kelly, I thought "This is no big deal. It's the same thing: Europeans oppressed blacks; blacks were over-whelmed; and blacks became slaves." Afterward then in class we were talking about how Kelly gives you the basic story as: A European society went over and took the blacks, and the blacks were helpless and became slaves and *accepted* it.

But the whole idea that they just were on the plantation and accepted life as that, is just false. You see it in Bennett. He uses personal histories like this one about a woman who had been a queen in her African nation, and how she would sing and think about going back to Africa, back to her homeland.

There was black culture, a lot through songs, a lot devel-oped through the field, a lot of escape methods were through songs that alerted people. There is not this acceptance on the blacks' part that "we're here and we are going to be slaves for the rest of our lives. Gee, darn, we'll have to wake up tomorrow morning and work." There was never a giving up. There were always escapes. There were always songs of the homeland. Kelly ignores that.

Zev is not confused by these comparisons, he is engaged by them. When he talks about the different accounts of slavery, he gestures and his voice is excited, accented. As he says, "This opens up history, you can see in to how it works."

Knowing One's Own Narratives: Asking the Question of Values

Though a junior, just beginning his American history course, Zev is beginning to understand—through his teachers' efforts to supplement the textbook—that there are different histories, told from different points of view. In this setting, Zev is pulled to realize that he has beliefs about history and about particular events. When, several months later, he "gets to" the Civil War and Reconstruction, he returns to his earlier efforts at interpreting the Edisto freedmen's letter with new insight.

Zev: We talked about how every time the blacks gained anything, it gets described like only by the help of the whites. The Emancipation Proclamation is only by the help of the whites. The Brown versus the School Board is only because of the whites fighting for black rights. There's this idea that blacks themselves can't do it. But to say that a culture cannot survive without giving it the chance to act freely is again choosing your history.

Interviewer: You've now been through a very different way of looking at the history of blacks in American history. I wonder what that makes you think about the history you imagined for the Edisto Island letter.

Zev: I did not believe, I guess, in my true heart, that blacks could have done that by themselves, given the circumstances. We are taught that blacks were given no education. From today, I learned to say—No. I still don't know. Perhaps there was white help. But that's not what's at issue. The point is that the blacks wanted to make a document, wanted to actually fight for something themselves. The point is that they were people just like the Puritans who fled from England who were looking for freedom. Never mind the given circumstances. They were a people looking for freedom.

So now I think that what I would be most interested in is not how the letter was written, but the ideas, the frustration, the real work of that letter.

I remember thinking, "Why would they want land so much, like before rights or education?" But now I think I would reverse that, in that land means they're free. Education means they're able to speak or write, but it's the very beginning to own something. Skills are for later. You know what I mean?

I don't think we as whites can see that easily, because we own our radios, we own our houses, and we own our freedom.

Finding and Pursuing a Historical Question

Zev "walked into" the church he imagined on Edisto Island. There he learned something about the place of entry and empathy in doing history. But he also formulated a question: It is a question about the difference between what he calls "the freedom of law" and "the freedom to live." In thinking about it, he comments:

> It is strange. The Puritans left England to get away from just the same thing. They hated the laws about who could use the land for what, they wanted religious freedom. They come here, they establish their "city on the hill" and they do the same thing to other people.

He senses that this is an old, a recurrent, and a troubling side of American history. But as he would be the first to argue, it is not enough just to imagine or to speculate. To do history is also to pursue an idea, to fit it out with facts, to test it, and to ask what it means.

Luckily for Zev, his history class permits this pursuit. In the simplest sense, he acquires the knowledge of events and people that he wanted when he first looked at the Edisto Island letter. He reads and talks about Jackson, the compromises over slavery, the outbreak of the Civil War, and the broken course of Reconstruction. But he gets more than the chronology. Zev is often asked to be a historian—making his own sense out of an array of texts, documents, and ideas that come up in class discussion. He also has the chance to cut a path of inquiry. Often, when there is an assignment, he has the latitude to choose among topics or to shape how he answers. As a result, he returns time and time again to the question of conflicting visions of freedom. Several weeks after reading the Edisto Island letter, he writes about the differences between black and white abolitionists, pushing his ideas further (see Figure 1).

Still later, as part of his final exam, Zev prepares to write

Figure 1

White abolitionists viewed slavery as a huge sin against the prized "rugged individualism" of the day. Slavery was like asylums and penitentiaries, a system that whites wanted to reform, however, they were not ready to deal with the consequences and general strife of the mass freeing of slaves. Whites saw slavery as the sin that must be avoided instead of a step on the long road to black equality.

Black abolitionists, such as Frederick Douglas, realized their differences with white abolitionists. Douglas said, "We assert that the man who has suffered wrong should be the man to demand justice — that the man struck is the man to cry out — and that the man who has suffered the cruel pangs of slavery must advocate liberty. We must be our own advocates + representatives, not alone, but independent, not separate from, but in connection with our white friends." Douglas' view came from the fact that he was a freed slave and knew the hardships of slavery that no white abolitionist would ever know.... Black abolitionists both realized + accepted that there was bound to be bloodshed and struggle if they were to succeed. Douglas said, "If there is no struggle, there is no progress." ....

The vast difference of Black + White abolitionists of the mid 1800's centered on their ideas of how to go about the issue of slavery. Whites took a primarily passive approach, content to wait for gradual change. While their intentions were not totally egalitarian. Blacks, on the other hand, delt with the present situation + constantly urged slaves to help themselves take the first steps toward freedom.

---

an essay about the place of minorities in American history. When the exam comes, there is no such question. The closest question is one about the history of the divisions between North and South. Zev remakes it, using it as a place to question what he now thinks of as the too simple contrast between the anti-slavery North and the pro-slavery South. In so doing, he revisits his idea of the difference between an endorsement of freedom as "right" and the willingness to seek it in everyday forms for the millions of black slaves living in the United States (see Figure 2).

He discusses Bleeding Kansas, the fights over the election of 1860, the violence of John Brown, and the Civil War. We

---

Figure 2

... But the puritans lacked their purity. In 1643 they became part of the triangular slave trade that traveled to Africa, The new World, + Britan. So they were indirectly involved in bringing slaves to the New World. This is the point that must be made clear. From the beginning, the North deplored slavery, but it was the institution, not the human sacrifice they detested. Northerners always spoke against slavery, but when push came to shove, they always had a vested interest in it ... By the early 1800's the North found themselves compromising on the issue of slavery during the Missouri Compromise of 1820. By the mid -1800's, The Compromise of 1850, engineered by Henry Clay, forced the non-slave North to tighten + start enforcing the Fugitive Slave Law, which compromised the priviously "Entitled freedom" of blacks in the North, read a quote from Robert Penn Warren about the Civil War. In it he talks about the danger of packaging history for your own needs. He says the South excuses its injustices by claiming to be at the mercy of its history. And the North, seeing itself as just and fair, excuses itself from the hard facts of its history.

In these ways, Zev makes a project out of the question of freedom. He collects the facts that help him to understand it. He talks and writes about it, trying to come at it from different vantage points. At the end of studying Reconstruction, in a discussion, Zev comes back to the Edisto Island letter:

Now I see it stands for a hundred, maybe thousands of events, most of them we don't know because they didn't have letters with them. Now it says to me, we have a very long history of talking about freedom, but being involved in slavery. It says that all we ever got from the Civil War was the freedom of laws. Freedom from the whip, but freedom to work as sharecroppers.

Coming face to face with Penn Warren, Zev recognizes why any kind of full history does not come out of textbooks. He comments:

Events alone don't make me excited. I don't care about the Missouri Compromise, who cares about Henry Clay, what does Bleeding Kansas have to do with today? What you get out of Penn Warren is an understanding of how those events shape what people will say in history class, "We freed the Blacks. . . . We gave them jobs. . . . They could be farmers." But the truth of the matter is, these kids have been taught to find comfortable ways to view our own often unkind history. ■

CHAPTER 5

A Conclusion and a Challenge

What is to be learned from these diverse experiences? What do Debbie's and J.J.'s skepticism about history as a study of real human experience, about the historian as creative writer, suggest is wrong with current methods of teaching history? What does their obvious talent for narrative and questioning suggest about the potential for new approaches to teaching them history? What can we learn from the image of Zev struggling with the Edisto letter and, with limited background, re-creating a plausible narrative not only of its authors' circumstances but of their innermost thoughts? Or from Zev fleshing out his ideas with facts and different analyses? What can we learn from Mr. J., Zev's high school teacher, who regularly confronts his students with alternative historical narratives and provokes them to judge for themselves? We learn, I believe, new possibilities for teaching at both the secondary and collegiate levels. Debbie, J.J., and Zev show us an untapped potential. Mr. J. shows us it can be done at the high school level.

The point here is not that my particular view of history must be accepted. Other capable and respected historians may dispute my characterizationof history as narrative, may be appalled at my insistence that the historian's experience profoundly shapes the history he or she writes. All this, too, is part of historical debate, part of the competing narrative of the craft itself. What is important is that we be self-reflective about that craft, and that we make that reflection part of what students learn and puzzle over. And, I would argue, that we do this best when we present them with the raw materials of history or of historical debate. Primary documents can provide students a basis for developing fresh interpretations, for writing new narratives about historical problems. Alternative historical texts force them to make choices among competing narratives written by others. In either case they are challenged not only to think for themselves but to think creatively.■

References

Bender, Thomas. 1986. "Holes and Parts: The Need for Synthesis in American History." *Journal of American History.* 73 (June): 120–136.

Boorstin, Daniel and Ruth Boorstin. 1987. *Hidden History.* New York: Harper and Row.

Bruner, Jerome. 1986. *Actual Minds, Possible Worlds.* Cambridge, Mass.: Harvard University Press.

Cheney, Lynne. 1987. *American Memory: A Report on the Humanities in the Nation's Public Schools.* Washington, D.C.: National Endowment for the Humanities.

Crick, Francis. 1988. *What Mad Pursuit: A Personal View of Scientific Discovery.* New York: Basic Books, Inc.

Foner, Eric. 1988. *Reconstruction: America's Unfinished Revolution, 1863–877.* New York: Harper and Row.

Gee, J..P. 1988. *The Legacies of Literacy: From Plato to Friere through Harvey Graff.* Cambridge, Mass.: Harvard Education Review.

Graff, Henry F. 1985. *America: The Glorious Republic.* Revised edition. Boston: Houghton Mifflin.

Graff, G. 1987. *Professing Literature: An Institutional History.* Chicago: University of Chicago Press.

Gruber, Howard. 1981. *Darwin on Man.* Chicago: The University of Chicago Press.

Hirsch, Bette. 1989. *Languages of Thought.* New York: College Entrance Examination Board.

Hirsch, Eric D. 1987. *Cultural Literacy: What Every American Needs to Know.* Boston: Houghton Mifflin.

Keller, Evelyn Fox. 1983. *Feeling for the Organism: The Life and Work of Barbara McClintock.* San Francisco: W. H. Freeman.

Krashen, Stephen. 1981. *Second Language Acquisition and Second Language Learning.* Oxford: Pergamon Press.

Labov, W. 1972. "The Transformation of Experience" in *Narrative Syntax: Language in the Inner City.* Philadelphia: University of Pennsylvania Press.

Mestre, Jose and Jack Lochead. 1990. *Academic Preparation in Science*. Second edition. New York: College Entrance Examination Board.

Molinsky, Steven and Bill Bliss. 1980. *Side by Side: English Grammar Through Guided Conversation*. Englewood Cliffs, N.J.: Prentice-Hall.

National Council of Teachers of Mathematics. 1989. *New Directions for Elementary School Mathematics: 1989 Yearbook*. Paul Trafton, 1989 yearbook editor; Albert Shulte, general yearbook editor. Reston, Va.: NCTM.

Perkins, David N. 1983. *The Mind's Best Work: A New Psychology of Creative Thinking*. Cambridge, Mass.: Harvard University Press.

Polanyi, Livia. 1982. *Telling the American Story: A Structural and Cultural Analysis of Conversational Storytelling*. Norwood, N.J.: Ablex Publishing.

Ravitch, Diane. 1987. *What Do Our 17-year-olds Know?: A Report on the First National Assessment of History and Literature*. New York: Harper and Row.

Resnick, Lauren. 1987. *Education and Learning to Think*. Washington, D.C.: National Academy Press.

Resnick, Lauren and Leopold Klopfer, eds. 1989. *Toward the Thinking Curriculum: Current Cognitive Research*. 1989 Yearbook of the Association of Supervision and Curriculum Development. Alexandria, Va.: ASCD.

Ricoeur, Paul. 1965. *History and Truth*. Evanston, Ill.: Northwestern University Press.

—1984. *Time and Narrative*. 3 volumes. Chicago: University of Chicago Press.

Silver, Edward A., 1990. *Thinking Through Mathematics*. New York: College Entrance Examination Board.

Wilder, Jacob, Robert Ludlum, and Harriet McCune Brown, eds. 1990. *America's Story*. Fifth edition. Boston: Houghton Mifflin.

Wolf, Dennie. 1987. *Reading Reconsidered: Literacy and Literacies in High School*. New York: College Entrance Examination Board.

Woodward, C. Vann. 1989. *The Future of the Past*. New York: Oxford University Press.

8107